Ralph Masiello's ALIEN DRAWING BOOK

ini Charlesbridge

For the DeGaetano aliens: Justin, Zachary, Michael Jr., A. J., Michael Sr., and Yolanda, who patiently await the arrival of the mother ship. And for John and Lauryn Gallagher, an amazing brother and sister team traveling through the mysteries of intergalactic time and space.

Also in this series:

Ralph Masiello's Ancient Egypt Drawing Book

Ralph Masiello's Bug Drawing Book

Ralph Masiello's Christmas Drawing Book

Ralph Masiello's Dinosaur Drawing Book

Ralph Masiello's Dragon Drawing Book

Ralph Masiello's Fairy Drawing Book

Ralph Masiello's Farm Drawing Book

Ralph Masiello's Halloween Drawing Book

Ralph Masiello's Ocean Drawing Book

Ralph Masiello's Robot Drawing Book

Other books illustrated by Ralph Masiello:

The Dinosaur Alphabet Book

The Extinct Alphabet Book

The Flag We Love

The Frog Alphabet Book

The Icky Bug Alphabet Book

The Icky Bug Counting Book

The Mystic Phyles: Beasts

The Skull Alphabet Book

The Yucky Reptile Alphabet Book

Cuenta los insectos

Published by Charlesbridge
85 Main Street
Watertown, MA 02472
(617) 926-0329
www.charlesbridge.com

At the time of publication, any URLs printed in this book were accurate and active. Charlesbridge and the author are not responsible for the content or accessibility of any URL.

Library of Congress Cataloging-in-Publication Data
Names: Masiello, Ralph, author.
Title: Ralph Masiello's alien drawing book.
Other titles: Alien drawing book.
Description: Watertown, MA : Charlesbridge, [2019]
Identifiers: LCCN 2018037334 (print) | LCCN 2019004428 (ebook) |
ISBN 9781607347484 (ebook) | ISBN 9781607346968 (ebook pdf) |
ISBN 9781570917691 (reinforced for library use) |
ISBN 9781570917707 (soft cover)
Subjects: LCSH: Extraterrestrial beings in art–Juvenile literature. |
   Outer space–In art–Juvenile literature. | Drawing–Technique–Juvenile
   literature.
Classification: LCC NC825.E88 (ebook) | LCC NC825.E88 M37 2019 (print) |
   DDC 743/.89001942–dc23
LC record available at https://lccn.loc.gov/2018037334

Printed in China
(hc) 10 9 8 7 6 5 4 3 2 1
(sc) 10 9 8 7 6 5 4 3 2 1

Illustrations done in mixed media
Display type set in Couchlover, designed by Chank, Minneapolis, Minnesota;
   text type set in Goudy Old Style
Color separations by Colourscan Print Co Pte Ltd, Singapore
Printed by 1010 Printing International Limited in Huizhou, Guangdong, China
Production supervision by Brian G. Walker
Designed by Susan Mallory Sherman & Jacqueline N. Cote

Greetings, Artists!

Hello, humans,

Here on my planet, far, far away, in another part of the galaxy, we LOVE to draw! I know that you humans love to draw as well! In this book, I will show you how to draw some of my other galactic space-traveling friends. From Sluggo-Blob to the more familiar Greens and Grays, you will be able to create some fun and sometimes silly beings from your solar system and beyond.

Follow the simple steps in red to draw my alien friends. Then if you like, add some of the extra features, shown in blue, to your alien life-forms. And, for even more fun, you can mix parts from one alien with parts from another to create your own unearthly beings.

And remember . . . have fun!

Ralphoid the Green

Choose your tools

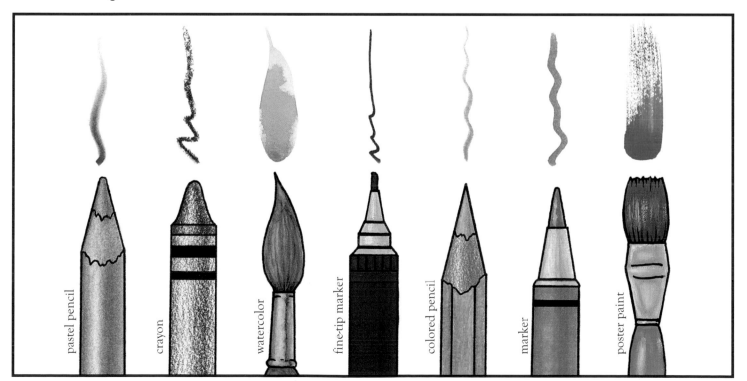

pastel pencil | crayon | watercolor | fine-tip marker | colored pencil | marker | poster paint

TOP SECRET

Alien Spare Parts Warehouse

Eyes

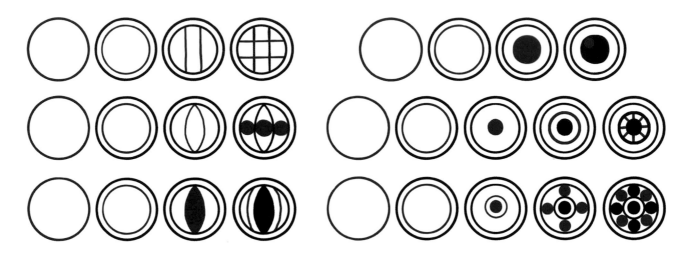

Antennae

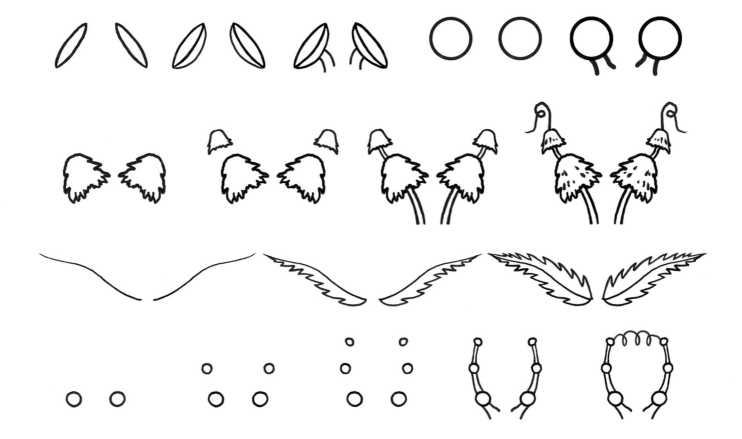

Robot Legs (two kinds)

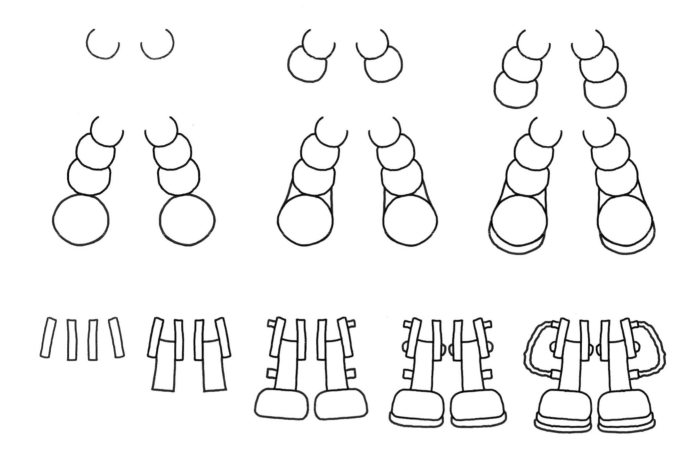

Tentacles

Hairy Arms with Bird Mouths

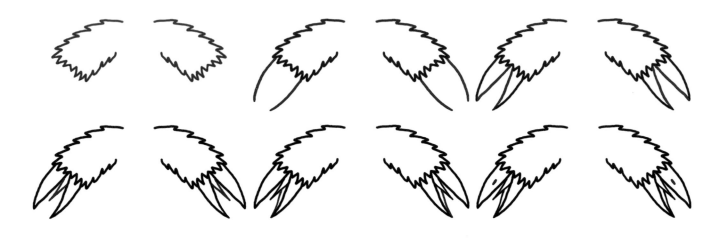

Webbed Feet

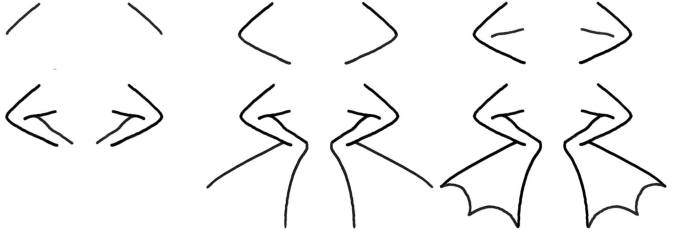

Robot Arms

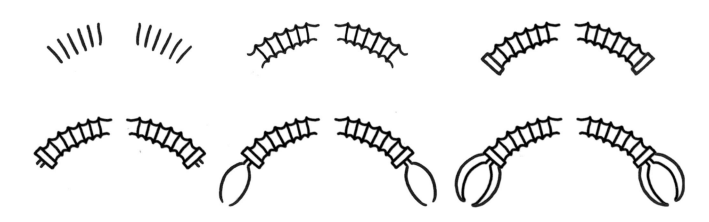

Wings

Mountain Valley

Flying Saucer

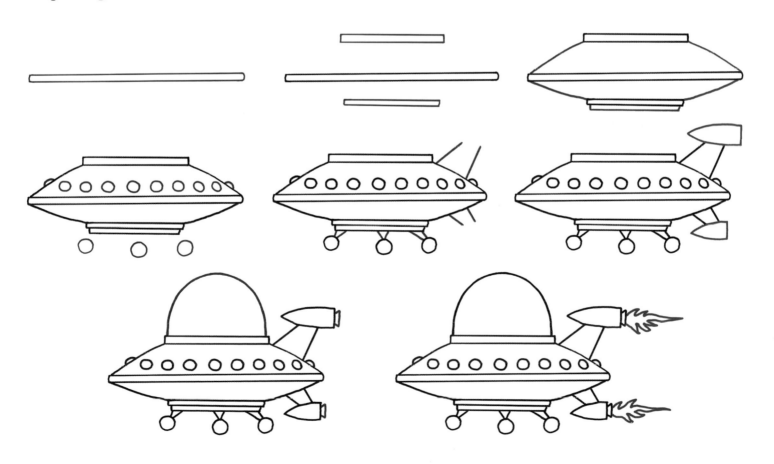

Sluggo-Blob of Saturn

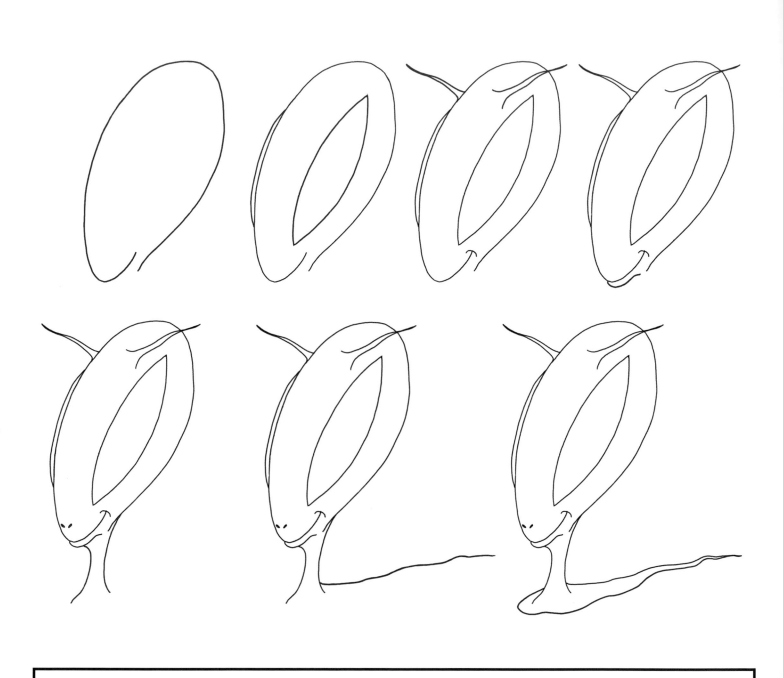

Goofy Goggles

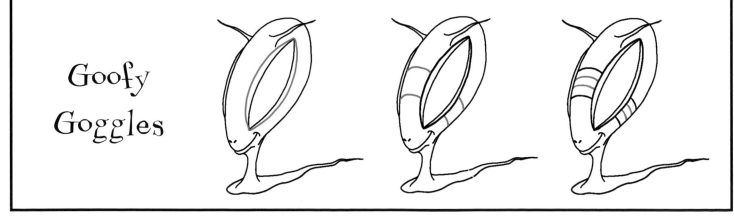

Saturn's silly Sluggo-Blob is slowly slithering.

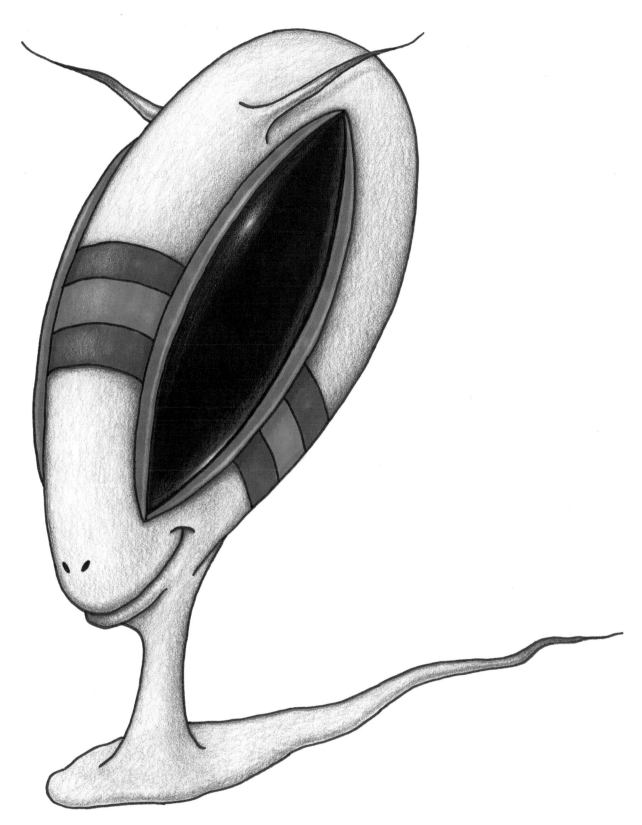

colored pencil

Ursula from Uranus

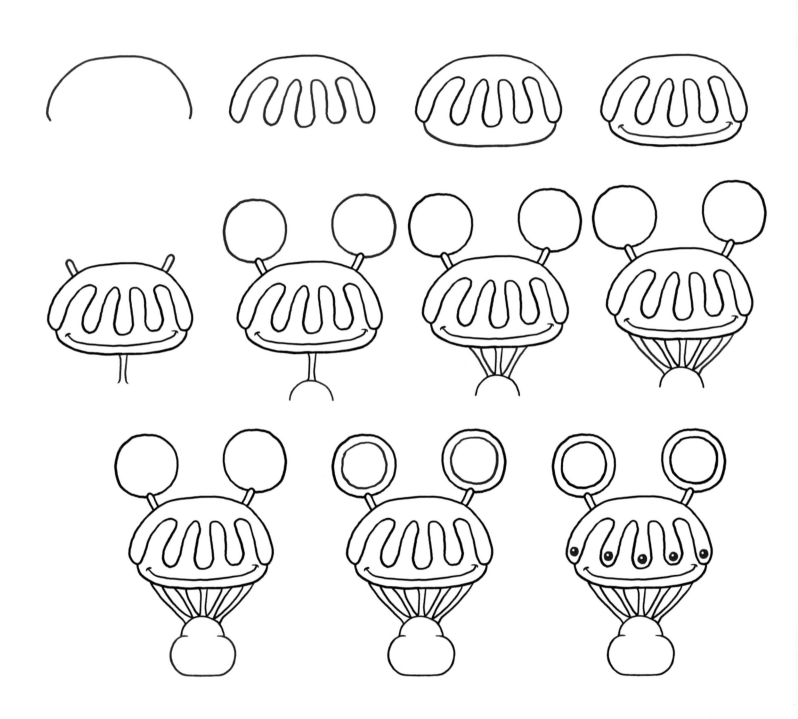

Remember to visit the Alien Spare Parts Warehouse
to complete your alien being!

marker and watercolor

Pat from Pluto

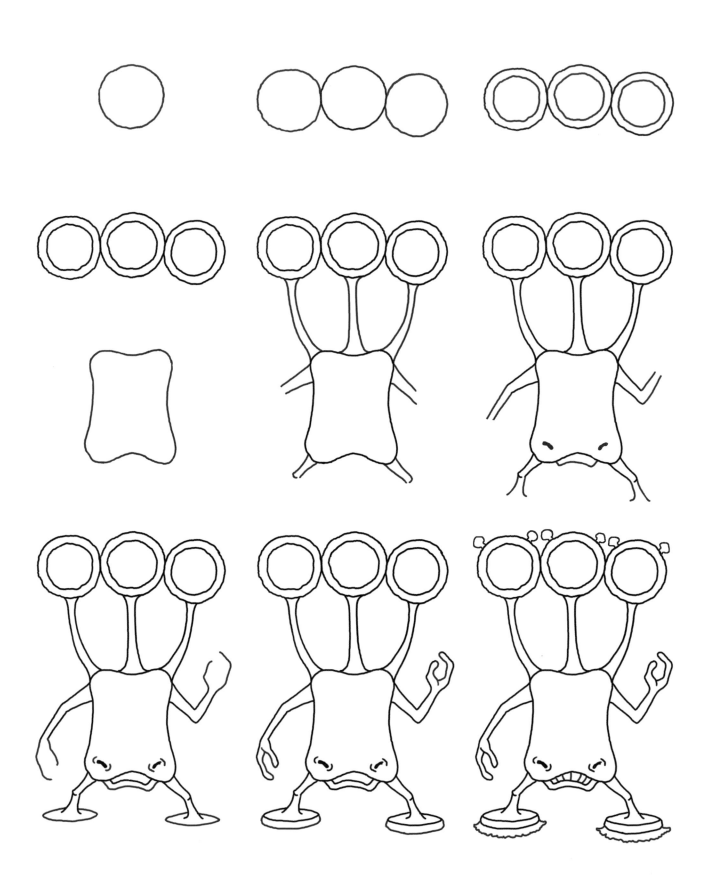

The "eyes" have it.

marker

Melvin on the Moon

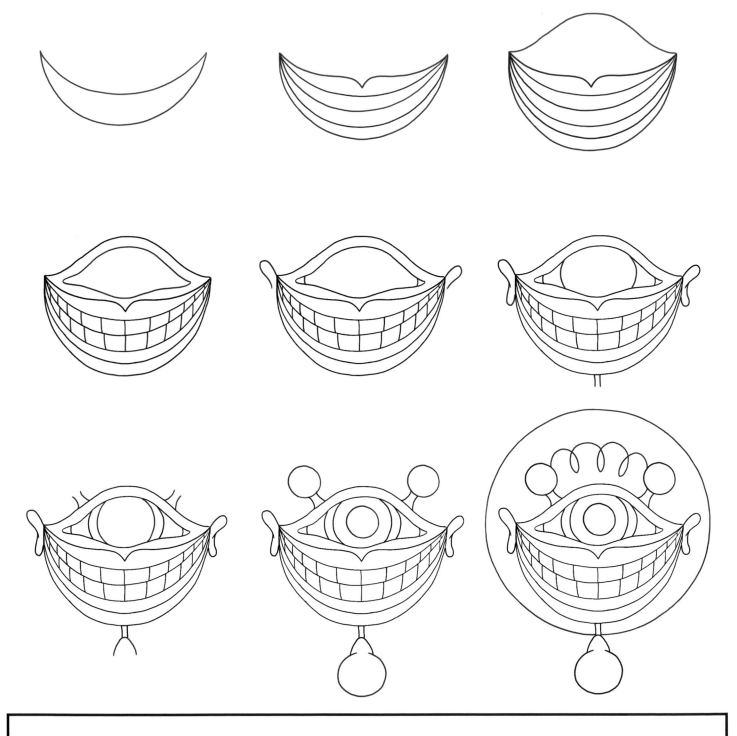

Belt and Buckle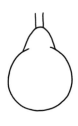

My, what large teeth you have.

marker and watercolor

—Mustache Man of Mercury—

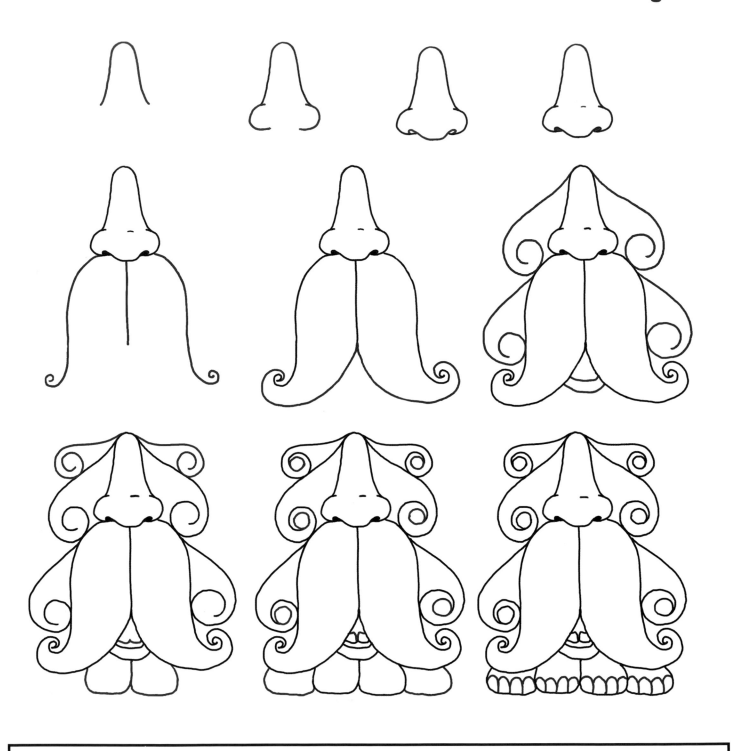

Craters

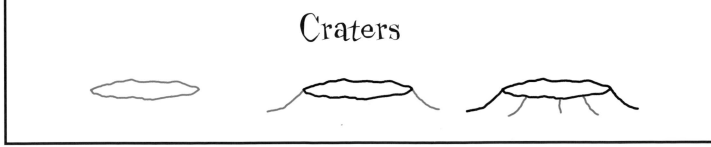

Who has a hairbrush I can borrow?

pastel, marker, and poster paint

Multimouthed Martian

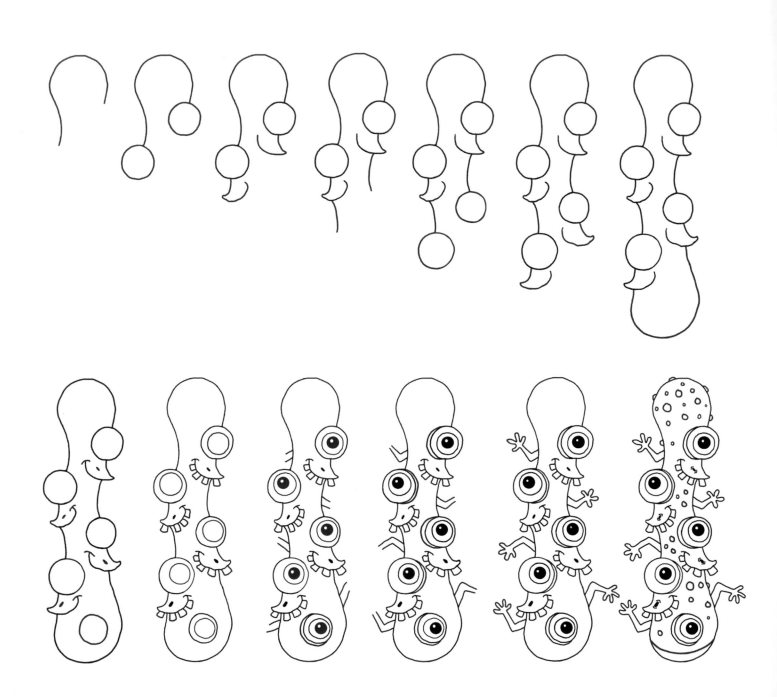

Stars and Moon

Turn up the music!
It's time for a Martian dance party!

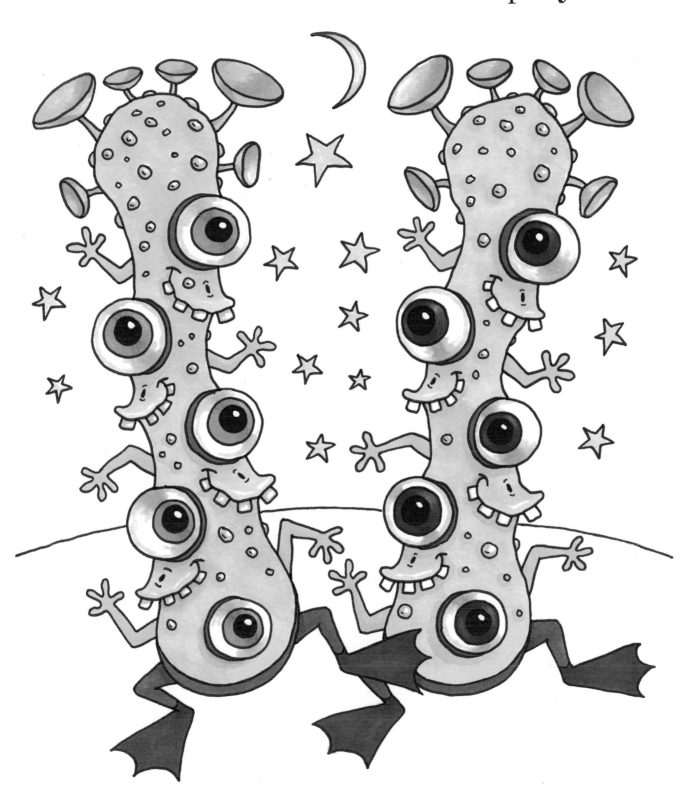

marker and poster paint

Noodly Newt of Neptune

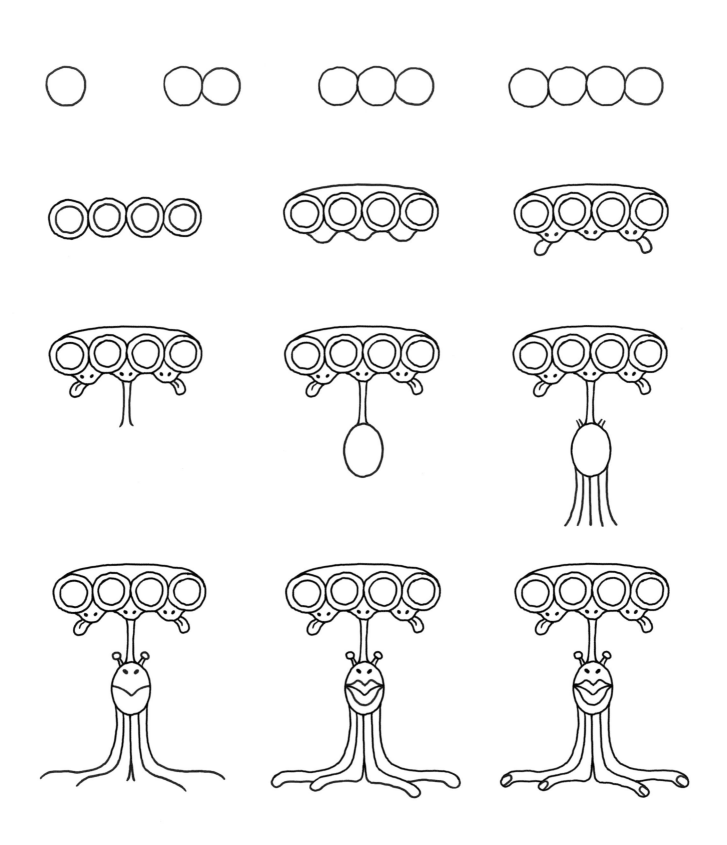

Drawing tentacles is a test of artistic talent!

colored pencil and marker

Jabber-Jaw of Jupiter

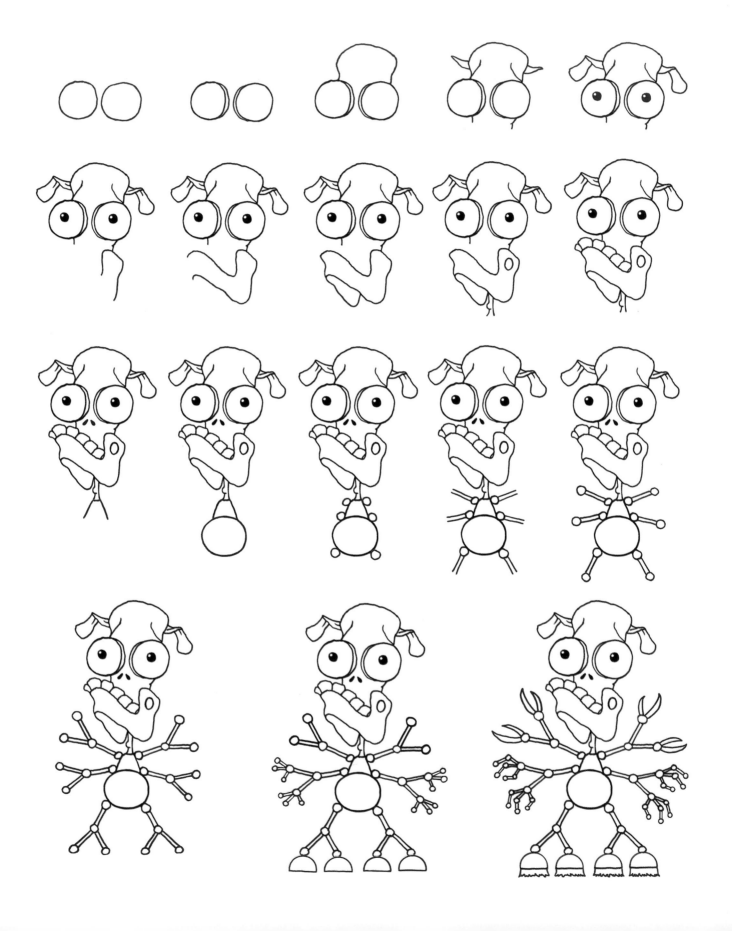

Being in a book makes me jittery!

crayon and marker

Green and Gray Galaxians

Galactic art adventures await!

marker and colored pencil

Vera from Venus

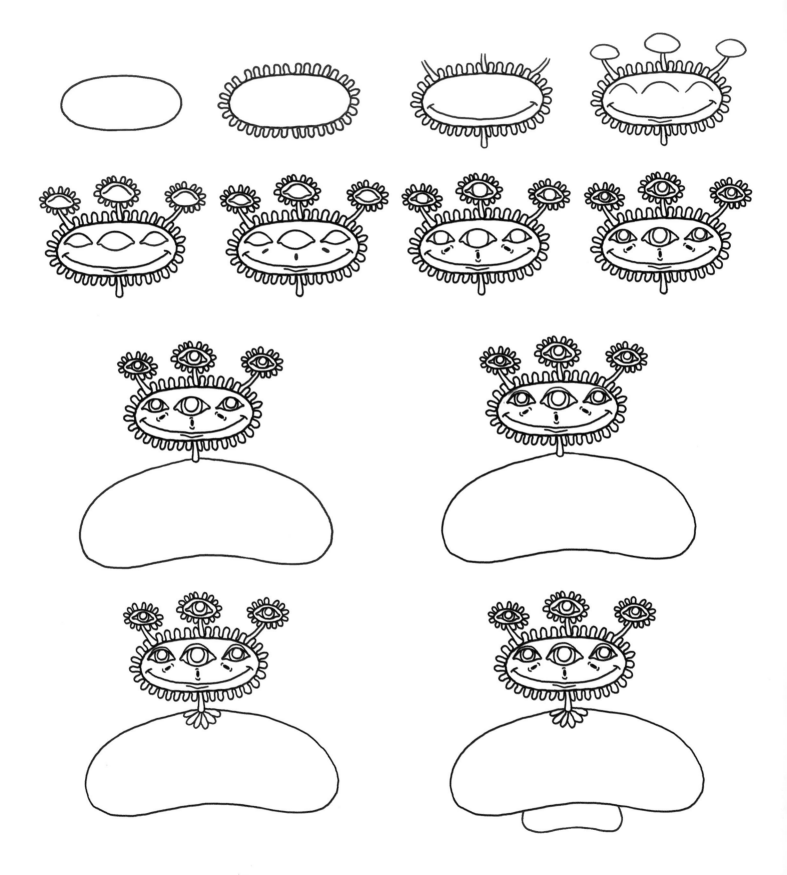

Add some windows to carry some friends!

Carpooling the Venutian way!

marker, colored pencil, and crayon

Intergalactic Gathering
Draw an intergalactic meeting of great friends!

marker, pastel, watercolor, poster paint, and colored pencil

Alien Resources

Now that you have embarked on your artistic quest to discover strange and unusual intergalactic life-forms, why not read some fun books and visit some cool websites about aliens!

Books for Kids, Parents, and Teachers

Fearing, Mark. *Earthling!* New York: Chronicle, 2012.

Freedman, Claire. Illustrated by Ben Cort. *Aliens Love Underpants.* London: Simon & Schuster Children's, 2007.

Hoopmann, Kathy. *Of Mice and Aliens: An Asperger Adventure.* Philadelphia: Jessica Kingsley, 2001.

McElligott, Matthew. *Even Aliens Need Snacks.* New York: Walker, 2012.

McNamara, Margaret. Illustrated by Mark Fearing. *The Three Little Aliens and the Big Bad Robot.* New York: Schwartz & Wade, 2011.

Scieszka, Jon. Illustrated by Lane Smith. *Baloney (Henry P.).* New York: Puffin, 2005.

Whelon, Chuck. *Alien Invasion! Mazes.* New York: Dover, 2010.

Websites

The Aliens Have Landed!
https://www.poetry4kids.com/poems/the-aliens-have-landed/#Uh9C-5Ksim4
Fun alien poetry by Kenn Nesbitt at his website Poetry4kids.

Bob the Alien's Tour of the Solar System
https://www.bobthealien.co.uk
Fun and interesting facts about our solar system and beyond.

"It's a Bird, It's a Plane, It's an Alien Spaceship?"
https://www.dogonews.com/2012/10/27/its-a-bird-its-a-plane-its-an-alien-spaceship
An article by Meera Dolasia, *DOGO News*, October 27, 2012.

"How Would We React to Finding Aliens?"
https://news.nationalgeographic.com/2018/02/how-would-people-react-alien-life-discovery-aaas-space-science
An article by Nadia Drake, *National Geographic*, February 16, 2018.

NASA Kids' Club
https://www.nasa.gov/kidsclub
Space activities and games.

An Alien Mask to Print Out and Color
http://www.studyvillage.com/attachments/9179-alien-mask-printable-coloring-page-for-kids
Downloadable from Study Village.